NATIONAL GEOGRAPHIC

ON ASSIGNMENT

Surviving
Volcanoes
and Glaciers

Rebecca L. Johnson

PICTURE CREDITS
Cover (background) T. Kitchin/V. Hurst/Photo Researchers; cover (bottom left) G. Brad Lewis/The Stone Collection/Getty Images; cover (bottom right), pages 2–3, 4 (left), 19 (left) Carsten Peter/National Geographic Image Collection; cover (back) Wedigo Ferchland/Bruce Coleman Inc.; pages 22–23 AFP/Corbis; page 2 (left) G. Brad Lewis/Science Photo Library/Photo Researchers; page 4 (right) EyeWire/Getty Images; page 5 (background), 30 PhotoDisc/Getty Images; pages 6–7 Chris Johns/National Geographic/Getty Images; page 8 courtesy of NASA; pages 9 (top), 10 (bottom), 11, 26 Roger Ressmeyer/Corbis; page 9 (bottom) Jose Honnorez/Bruce Coleman Inc.; page 10 (top) Douglas Peebles/Corbis; pages 1,13 courtesy of United States Geological Survey; page 14 (inset) Sime s.a.s./eStock Photography/Picture Quest; pages 14–15 Bernhard Edmaier/Science Photo Library/Photo Researchers; page 17 (top) Neil Rabinowitz/Corbis; page 17 (bottom), 19 (right), 20 (left) Ann Parks Hawthorne; page 18 David Vaughn/Science Photo Library/Photo Researchers; pages 20–21 Simon Fraser/Science Photo Library/Photo Researchers; page 23 (inset) Yann Arthus-Bertrand/Corbis; page 24 (top and bottom) Steve Winter/National Geographic Image Collection; pages 24–25 Morgun Bladid/National Geographic Image Collection.

ARTWORK
Linda Kelen

LOCATOR GLOBES
Mapping Specialists Limited

Produced through the worldwide resources of the National Geographic Society, John M. Fahey, Jr., President and Chief Executive Officer; Gilbert M. Grosvenor, Chairman of the Board; Nina D. Hoffman, Executive Vice President and President, Books and Education Publishing Group.

PREPARED BY NATIONAL GEOGRAPHIC SCHOOL PUBLISHING
Ericka Markman, Senior Vice President and President Children's Books and Education Publishing Group; Steve Mico, Senior Vice President, Publisher, Editorial Director; Marianne Hiland, Editorial Director; Jim Hiscott, Design Manager; Kristin Hanneman, Illustrations Manager; Matt Wascavage, Manager of Publishing Services; Sean Philpotts, Production Manager.

MANUFACTURING AND QUALITY MANAGEMENT
Christopher A. Liedel, Chief Financial Officer; Phillip L. Schlosser, Director; Clifton M. Brown III, Manager.

PROGRAM DEVELOPMENT
Kate Boehm Jerome

CONSULTANTS/REVIEWERS
Dr. James Shymansky, E. Desmond Lee Professor of Science Education, University of Missouri-St. Louis
Glen Phelan, science writer, Palatine, Illinois

BOOK DEVELOPMENT
Thomas Nieman, Inc.

BOOK DESIGN
Herman Adler Design

Published by the National Geographic Society
1145 17th Street, N.W.
Washington, D.C. 20036-4688

ISBN-13: 978-0-7922-8448-2
ISBN-10: 0-7922-8448-8

Third Printing June 2012
Printed in Canada.

Steam rises from the point where hot lava meets the ocean.

Contents

**Exploring the ceiling
of a glacial ice cave**

A scientist on a volcano

A climber inside a glacier

Introduction

One False Step . . .

Dressed in a heatproof suit, a volcano researcher inches closer to the crater's edge. Just a few meters away, red-hot lava is shooting skyward. One false step and he could tumble into the fiery heart of this erupting volcano.

Half a world away, a team of scientists crosses an Alaskan glacier. The team leader suddenly stops. "Crevasse!" she calls out. A **crevasse** is a deep crack in the ice. A step in the wrong direction could mean a serious fall.

At first, you might think volcanoes and glaciers have nothing in common. One is searing hot. The other is frozen solid. When a volcano **erupts**, the action is fast and furious. Glaciers creep along.

Yet volcanoes and glaciers are alike in a big way. These powerful forces of fire and ice constantly reshape the surface of our planet. In this book, you'll go on assignment with scientists who study volcanoes and glaciers in some of the world's most extreme environments. Get ready to feel the heat and brave the cold!

Mountains of Fire

On the island of Hawaii, melted rock from deep underground surges out of a crack in the Kilauea volcano. Glowing orange-red, the lava flows down to the ocean. It meets the water with a loud hiss of steam. The lava cools quickly, turning into rock.

Hawaii

Kilauea

Pacific Ocean

Volcanoes create new land by bringing melted rock from deep inside Earth to the surface. But volcanoes can also destroy. A volcanic eruption can blow the top off a mountain. It can spit out tons of ash and hot, poison gas. It can bury roads and towns under thick lava.

Flowing lava reaches the ocean in Hawaii.

By studying volcanoes, scientists learn what's happening inside our planet. They also draw conclusions about how Earth has changed over time.

Scientists who study volcanoes are known as **volcanologists**. They travel all over the world to do their work. That's because volcanoes are found on every continent. But they are clustered in certain places. Let's see why.

Earth's outermost layer is the **crust**. The crust is made up of about 20 large **plates** that fit together like pieces of a jigsaw puzzle. Beneath the crust lies a layer called the **mantle**. The upper mantle near the crust contains some melted rock. Where there are weak spots in the crust, melted rock from the mantle can push through to the surface. When it does, a volcano can form.

So where are the weak spots? Most are found where the plates of the crust come together. Volcanoes form along these "seams."

Volcano Watch

National Geographic Society writer Noel Grove went on assignment to learn more about volcanoes. He joined scientists from all over the world in studying these mountains of fire.

Noel discovered that volcanologists use some high-tech tools to keep an eye on volcanoes. These tools let them know when a volcano might be about to do something interesting.

From space, **satellites** take detailed pictures of Earth's surface. By studying satellite pictures, scientists can spot changes in volcanoes. These changes might not be visible from the ground.

When the land around a volcano starts to shake, it's a clue. Something is happening deep inside. Volcanologists keep track of this shaking with detectors called **seismometers**.

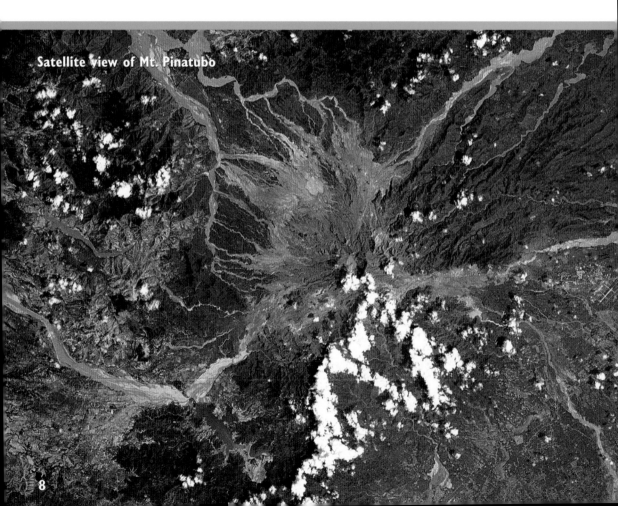

Satellite view of Mt. Pinatubo

On Mt. Pinatubo in the Philippines, Noel saw how volcanologists place seismometers in the ground around the volcano. The detectors pick up the slightest movements in the ground. When the volcano starts to shake a lot, an eruption is possible. Seismometers helped scientists predict one of Pinatubo's largest-ever eruptions in 1991.

Volcanologists discuss a printout of seismic activity.

Scientists place a seismometer near the base of a volcano.

A helicopter carries scientists up to a volcano's crater during an eruption.

Wearing gas masks, scientists hike up the side of a steaming volcano.

At the Crater's Edge

Long-distance tools, such as satellites and seismometers, can tell scientists a lot. But to get some kinds of information, people must study volcanoes up close. Sometimes they are flown in helicopters up to the **crater** at the very top of a volcano. In other cases, the only way up is on foot.

Once on the volcano, researchers don't waste any time gathering what they need. Conditions inside the mountain can change quickly, often without warning. What seems safe one moment can be deadly the next.

Researchers collect samples of the gases puffing out of a volcano's crater or through cracks in its sides. Back in a lab, they test the samples. They try to figure out what kinds of gases are present. The mix of gases coming out of a volcano gives clues on what's happening inside.

Scientists collect lava, too. On Hawaii's Kilauea, Noel followed U.S. Geological Survey researcher Tari Mattox. They traveled across the volcano's steaming surface, where fresh lava flowed. Noel thought the lava looked like cherry syrup. But Tari explained that it was incredibly hot. It's over 2000°F (1093°C)! To get a sample, Tari slipped on a heatproof helmet and special gloves. She stepped carefully as she snagged a glob of fresh lava on a metal rod.

Back in her lab, Tari would figure out the mix of **minerals** in the lava. That information could tell her if anything was changing inside Kilauea.

Scientists must find ways to beat the heat to collect lava samples.

Into the Inferno

It's one thing to sample lava flowing peacefully down Kilauea's sides. It's quite another to grab some from a volcano that's erupting violently. When Sicily's Mt. Etna blew its top in July 2001, volcanologists from all over the world were there. Dressed in heatproof suits, some worked just an arm's length away from fiery lava fountains.

Searing heat is just one of the dangers the scientists faced. An erupting volcano also can cough out poison gas. It can hurl car-sized blobs of lava, called "bombs," high into the air. When they fall back to Earth, watch out!

Scariest of all, however, are **pyroclastic flows**. These fast-moving clouds of gas and dust are killers. They are so hot that they set fire to everything in their path. From a safe distance, Noel Grove once watched a pyroclastic flow form on a volcano. It started as a grey bulge near the peak. Seconds later it had blossomed into a deadly cloud 65 meters (213 feet) high. Then the cloud went screaming down the mountainside.

Cool Fix! National Geographic photographer Carsten Peter was at the scene when Mt. Etna erupted in 2001. To protect himself from scorching heat and deadly gases, he wore a gas mask and a heatproof helmet. To keep his cameras safe, he carried them in special protective bags. Still, the heat took a toll. He had lots of repairs!

Is working on an erupting volcano worth the risks? Most volcanologists would say YES! They know their job can be dangerous. It's also exciting. And there's just no other way to collect the kind of information they can get at the crater's edge.

What scientists are learning about volcanoes helps us understand the powerful forces at work inside Earth. Wherever melted rock oozes, bubbles, or spurts up from the mantle, new rock and new land form. Scientists know that this process created Earth's first continents and sea floors 4 billion years ago. And the same process has been reshaping Earth ever since.

Pyroclastic flow of fast-moving, hot gases and dust on Mayon Volcano, Philippines

Rivers of Ice

Glaciers are enormous slow-moving masses of ice. As they creep along, glaciers grind down mountains and carve out valleys. Where glaciers meet the sea, they give birth to icebergs.

Glacial ice meets water in Argentina.

Glaciers form where more snow falls each year than melts away. Over time, the snow collects and compacts. Slowly, it turns into ice many meters—even a few kilometers—thick.

Many of the world's glaciers are found among high mountain peaks.

...become icebergs.

In North America, Alaska is home to about 48,270 square kilometers (18,637 square miles) of glacier ice. Earth's largest glaciers, known as **ice sheets**, cover vast areas of land in Greenland and Antarctica.

Glacier scientists, or **glaciologists**, study glaciers to learn more about them. They learn how they have shaped Earth in the past and continue to shape it today. Like volcanoes, glaciers are a challenge to study. Glaciologists must brave bitter cold and fierce winds in far-away places. Sometimes, they walk a slippery line between life and death.

Checking Out Change

In their research, glaciologists try to answer questions about the world's great rivers of ice. Are glaciers getting thicker or thinner? Are they moving faster or slower? How are they being affected by changes taking place on Earth?

Like volcano scientists, glacier scientists use satellites to keep an eye on glaciers from space. They also take pictures of glaciers from airplanes. In Alaska, for example, researchers fly small planes over the mountains on a regular basis. They take pictures of glaciers from different angles. These **aerial photographs** form a sort of photo album. The photos help show how slow-moving glaciers are changing over time.

How? You probably don't notice how your face changes from day to day. But compare a picture taken two years ago with a current one. You'll see all sorts of changes.

The same is true for glaciers. A glacier might look pretty much the same from month to month. But when you compare aerial photos taken of that glacier over 5, 10, or 20 years, changes are easy to spot.

Getting There

Some kinds of information can only be collected by "being there." Getting to glaciers can be difficult. Some are tucked atop very high mountains. Others are in parts of the world where there are no roads, towns, or people—nothing but windswept ice and snow as far as the eye can see.

Small airplanes or helicopters carry teams of scientists to these glaciers, along with everything they need to set up a camp. The researchers may live and work on the glacier for many weeks. Their only contact with the outside world is through radio and satellite communications.

Can you imagine living in a tent on ice? Would you like to wake up every morning to below-zero temperatures? Or how about working in icy winds blowing 128 kph (80 mph)? Your bathroom might be just a hole in the snow surrounded by snow-bricks to block the wind!

The right-hand side of the glacier shows the path of retreating ice.

Field camp on an Antarctic glacier

Science on Ice

To learn how fast a glacier moves, researchers pound dozens of tall stakes into the ice. When they plant each stake, they record its exact location. They use a device called a GPS. A GPS uses satellites in space to figure out exactly where something is on Earth.

From time to time, the scientists go back to see how much the stakes have moved. They locate each stake and figure out its new position. Then they compare the original positions of the stakes with their new ones. This allows the researchers to figure out how fast the glacier is moving.

The movement of glaciers causes crevasses to form in the ice. Some crevasses are small and shallow. Others can be many meters deep. When working in crevassed areas, researchers may wear crash helmets and body harnesses. Team members are linked together by ropes tied to their harnesses. If someone slips into a crevasse, the rope will save her or him from falling in all the way.

Sometimes, researchers go into crevasses or caves in the ice on purpose. From inside the glacier they can see details about its structure that they can't see from the top. It's a cold—and sometimes dangerous—world to explore. But many would say it's one of the most beautiful, too.

Setting up a GPS on a glacier in Antarctica

Did you ever wonder why glaciers and icebergs look blue? When sunlight passes through thick chunks of ice, all the colors in the light are absorbed except blue. Since only blue light is reflected, the ice looks blue to our eyes.

Blue-ice glacier in Antarctica

Climbing inside a glacier cave

Going Deeper

Scientists keep track of how much snow falls onto a glacier each winter. They also figure out how much ice melts away or evaporates each summer. Using these measurements, they can tell if a glacier is getting thinner or thicker.

Scientists take cores from glaciers. An **ice core** is a long, round cylinder drilled from glacier ice. It can be many meters long. By studying gases and other substances trapped in ice cores, scientists gather clues about what Earth's climate was like thousands of years ago.

New technologies are helping scientists "see" under glaciers.

For example, radio waves are sent down through the ice. When the waves hit rock, they bounce back up through the ice to a receiver. The receiver creates a picture on a computer screen of the landscape beneath the ice.

As scientists explore glaciers from top to bottom, they learn how glaciers change our planet. They also discover how people may be changing glaciers.

A scientist cuts an ice core in Antarctica.

Satellite pictures, aerial photos, and direct measurements all show that in some parts of the world, glaciers are shrinking rapidly. Many scientists think this is caused by **global warming**, an increase in Earth's average surface temperature. There's pretty good evidence that global warming results when people add certain gases to the atmosphere. We do this when we burn huge amounts of coal, oil, and other fossil fuels.

If the enormous ice sheets that cover Greenland and Antarctica ever melt, even a little, they will add enormous amounts of water to the oceans. This could raise sea levels worldwide. Will it happen? Scientists don't know yet. They will keep studying these great rivers of ice to find an answer.

When Fire and Ice Meet

Volcanoes and glaciers are powerful forces on their own. Imagine what might happen if the two came together. The people who live in Iceland don't have to wonder—they know! On Iceland, fire and ice meet regularly—often with spectacular results.

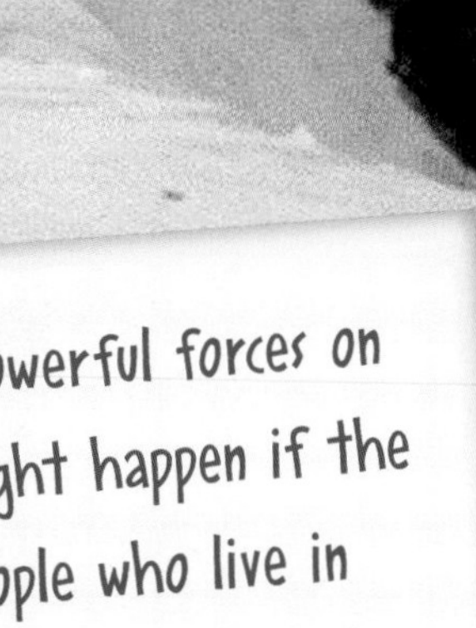

Asia

North America

Europe

Iceland

Atlantic Ocean

Volcanic eruption under a glacier in Iceland

Surtsey Island off Iceland

Iceland is surrounded by the cold water of the northern Atlantic Ocean. It lies right over a weak spot in Earth's crust. On this island country, volcanic activity is a part of everyday life.

If you walk across the Icelandic countryside, you'll see smoke and steam puffing from cracks in the ground. Sometimes, amazing eruptions occur. In 1963, an undersea volcano began erupting off Iceland's coast. It spouted so much lava that a new island was formed. The Icelanders called it Surtsey, after Surtur, the Norse god of fire.

In 1996, another huge volcanic eruption hit Iceland. This time, though, the action was not in the sea. It was right under the island's biggest glacier.

When hot lava met cold ice, great clouds of steam billowed high into the air. As the lava kept coming, the bottom of the glacier began to melt. Billions of liters of water streamed out from the melting glacier and formed a lake.

Scientists from all over the world watched. The lake grew larger. So much ice was melting that the lake water was rising 18 meters (60 feet) a day! After a while, the ice around the lake broke away, releasing a great flood.

The floodwaters swept away Iceland's longest bridge. They destroyed roads and power lines. After the flood, the land was littered with huge chunks of ice. No one was killed. But millions of dollars of damage had been done.

In Iceland, scientists can watch both volcanoes and glaciers. They can see how these forces have shaped the island for hundreds of thousands of years. Studying volcanoes and glaciers can be a dangerous business. But seeing the forces of fire and ice at work makes it all worthwhile.

Iceland's largest bridge was destroyed by the glacial flood.

A person is dwarfed by ice the flood left behind.

Investigating to Solve a Problem

Volcanologists wear heatproof suits when working near an erupting volcano. To create these special suits, researchers had to do a lot of work. They had to investigate what kinds of materials would work best. The material needed to reflect intense heat. It also had to be lightweight and flexible enough to wear.

In their investigations, researchers gathered data about the different kinds of materials. Then they carried out some tests. Over time they found the best material to use for making heatproof suits. This gear may not be very fashionable, but it does keep volcanologists safe.

When you investigate, you study something very closely. You collect detailed information that sometimes involves experiments. You learn by carefully observing what happens when you experiment. These observations can help you answer a question or solve a problem. Let's take a closer look at what investigating is all about.

Step 1 Ask a Question

Every day you face problems to solve at home and in school. Some are simple. Others take more work to figure out. When problems arise, the first step is to state the problem as a question. Every investigation begins with a question of some sort.

How Can I Beat the Heat?

Some friends are over to watch a video. For a snack you're making three frozen pizzas. You pop the first pizza in the oven. The timer goes off, and you take the pizza out of the oven. But the edges of the crust are burned! They must have gotten too hot. You don't want to make the same mistake again. So, state your problem as a question: How can I keep the edges of a pizza from getting burned?

Step 2 Gather Information

The second step in investigating is to gather information. Information is the key to answering your question. Sometimes, you can find information in books, magazines, or on the Internet. Parents and teachers can be good sources of information, too. Other times, a little experimenting may be in order.

What Could I Use That Will Help?

You're pretty sure the pizza crust burned because it got too hot. So how are you going to shield the other pizzas from the heat? You rummage through the kitchen drawers. Hey—aluminum foil! You know that aluminum foil can reflect heat. Maybe you could use it as a heat shield for pizza crust. You decide to experiment on the two pizzas left. The first one you cover completely with aluminum foil. On the second pizza, you just cover the outer edges. You pop the pizzas into the oven to bake.

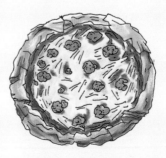

Step 3   Analyze the Data

The next step in investigating is to analyze the information you gathered. That means you try to make sense of the data. You think about how it relates to your question. Can the information give you the answer you need?

A Tale of Two Pizzas

The oven timer goes off. You peel back the aluminum foil from the pizza that was covered completely. The edge of the crust isn't burned! But the center of the pizza isn't cooked. It didn't get enough heat!

The other pizza looks perfect in the center—the cheese is golden brown. But what about the edges of the crust? You pull off the aluminum foil that covered them. Aha! Crisp but not burned—success!

Step 4   Draw a Conclusion

The last step in investigating is to draw a conclusion. Based on your analysis of your information—and the results of any experiments—you answer your question.

And the Answer Is ...

Using aluminum foil as a heat reflector on pizza worked. Covering the entire pizza, though, reflected too much heat. The center of the pizza didn't get hot enough to cook completely. But covering just the edges of the crust kept them from burning while the rest of the pizza baked to a lovely golden brown. Your investigation is complete!

Problem Solving on Your Own

Understand the Problem

Your group is in charge of gathering supplies for an art project. The class is making models of the different kinds of volcanoes you have been studying. You make a list of the supplies you will need: construction paper, marking pens, tape, scissors, and crayons. You go to your art teacher to get the supplies.

The art teacher has most of the supplies, but there is one problem. She has only half the number of scissors you need, and they are all left-handed. How will everyone in your class be able to work on this project? Will everyone be able to do the same thing? It's time to investigate and collect some information.

Find a Solution

Work with a group to figure out how to answer this question. Use the steps below to guide your investigation.

1 Ask a Question
2 Gather Information
3 Analyze the Data
4 Draw a Conclusion

Science Notebook

Fun Facts

• When Mt. Etna erupted in the summer of 2001, it spouted fountains of lava that soared 390 meters (1300 feet) up into the air.

• In 1883, the Indonesian volcano Krakatau erupted violently. The explosion was heard more than 4800 kilometers (about 3000 miles) away.

• Some of the best places for finding meteorites—chunks of metallic rock that fall to Earth from outer space—are on the windswept surfaces of glaciers in Antarctica.

A lava flow from Kilauea destroyed these cars.

Web Connection

If volcanoes have fired up your imagination, check out Volcano World at volcano.und.nodak.edu. You can see pictures of all the world's major volcanoes and even e-mail questions to a volcanologist.

Go behind the scenes with glaciologists working in Antarctica and Alaska by visiting www.glacier.rice.edu and www.crevassezone.org.

Take the Fire and Ice Challenge!

After you've had a chance to become well informed about these forces of fire and ice, choose a favorite volcano or glacier somewhere in the world. Then create a poster about it to share with your classmates.

Glossary

aerial photographs pictures taken of Earth's surface from an airplane or helicopter

crater bowl-shaped area around a volcano's opening

crevasse deep crack in glacier ice

crust Earth's outermost layer

erupt become violently active

glaciologists scientists who study glaciers

global warming increase in Earth's average surface temperature

ice core long cylinder drilled from a glacier

ice sheets Earth's largest glaciers

lava melted rock that surges up from the mantle and breaks through Earth's crust

mantle earth layer underneath the crust. The top part of the mantle contains nearly melted rock.

minerals naturally occurring solids, such as quartz or garnet

plates huge sections of Earth's crust; most volcanoes occur where plates meet

pyroclastic flows fast-moving clouds of volcanic matter that are hot enough to set things on fire

satellites high-tech instruments that orbit Earth; some satellites take detailed pictures of Earth's surface

seismometers instruments that detect vibrations in the ground

volcanologists scientists who study volcanoes

Index